THE DEATH PROJECT MANAGER

MORTALITY WORKBOOK

This workbook belongs to: _____

This document was last updated on: _____

info@deathprojectmanager.com | deathprojectmanager.com

The Death Project Manager Mortality Workbook

Copyright © 2021 Death Project Manager
All rights reserved

Author
Catherine

Design
Amy Burek

Printed at Chute Studio in Oakland, CA
First Edition
Fifth Printing
March 2024

info@deathprojectmanager.com | deathprojectmanager.com

TABLE OF CONTENTS

Welcome 4

Why This Workbook? 5

Before We Begin . . . . 6 - 8

Form Letter 9

Key Facts About You 10

Key Contacts in Case of Emergency . . . . 11 - 13

Funeral Invitation & Notification List . . . . 14 - 15

Important Documents . . . . 16 - 19

To Do List for Loved Ones . . . . 20 - 22

Social Media & Digital Assets . . . . 23 - 26

Pets 27

Decisions to Make, Discussions to Have . . . . 28 - 31

The Funeral . . . . 32 - 37

Closing Reflections . . . . 38 - 39

info@deathprojectmanager.com | deathprojectmanager.com

WELCOME

You're doing a brave thing in picking up this guide.

We believe that planning and logistics are expressions of care and compassion: it can be a final way to show the people who matter most to you, that you are thinking of their comfort during a challenging time.

It is also an act of compassion to yourself: the process helps clarify the aspects of your life that are important to you so you can spend more of your time on them.

It also helps you to spend more of your end-of-life enjoying life instead of making decisions.

This is an incredibly kind thing to do. 6 in 10 Americans do not have a will or living trust in place[1].

We're grateful to join you in finding a way to express your care.

This guide is meant to help you begin the process of reflecting on your values, the people who matter to you, and broadly what you would like to happen at the end of your life. This is meant to begin conversations and be a living document - a step towards articulating **what your loved ones should know before you go.**

We recommend reviewing and updating this information annually, to make sure it is as up to date as possible.

---

[1] www.aarp.org/money/investing/info-2017/half-of-adults-do-not-have-wills.html

WHY THIS WORKBOOK?

This workbook can help you to:

- Focus on what - and who - matters most to you
- Organize needed paperwork in case of emergency
- Articulate your values and reflect on ways to incorporate those values into your daily life
- Create a plan and support for your community during a difficult time

WHAT THIS WORKBOOK PROVIDES

- A guide to collecting important documents and information
- A space to reflect on your values and end of life wishes, as well as communicating those values to loved ones

WHAT DEATH PROJECT MANAGER CAN PROVIDE

- Coaching conversations with a Project Manager to keep you accountable for tracking down and condensing important information
- A resource to reflect on your mortality with a death-positive guide well-versed in green and non-traditional burial options
- Connections to service providers for legal, tax, and grief advice

Visit deathprojectmanager.com to access our coaching services or to purchase the full, electronic version of our Toolkit.

BEFORE WE BEGIN

Why did you purchase this guide? What do you hope to have in place when you finish this guide?

___

Where do you want to focus your energy with this project?

___

What or who motivates you?

___

If you get stuck, what do you want yourself to remember during this project?

_____
_____
_____
_____
_____
_____
_____
_____
_____
_____
_____
_____
_____
_____
_____

What memories do you have related to death?

_____
_____
_____
_____
_____
_____
_____
_____
_____
_____
_____
_____
_____
_____

Based on your previous experiences with death, what would you like to avoid in planning your legacy?

_____
_____
_____
_____
_____
_____
_____
_____
_____
_____
_____
_____
_____
_____

Based on your previous experiences with death, what moments of grace and kindness do you remember that you'd like to incorporate into your own planning?

_____
_____
_____
_____
_____
_____
_____
_____
_____
_____
_____
_____
_____
_____

FORM LETTER:
LETTING PEOPLE KNOW THIS DOCUMENT EXISTS

You are doing a kind thing in gathering this information for your loved ones.

Make sure they are aware this document exists. Use this form letter below as a template to let them know where to find this vital information.

> Hi [Loved One],
>
> I hope you're doing well.
>
> I wanted to let you know I've been doing contingency planning and have assembled a collection of important documents to have on hand in case of an emergency, or in case I pass suddenly.
>
> There is a binder and zine in the beige filing cabinet in my bedroom — check the first drawer for the binder with "In Case of Emergency" on the cover.
>
> Don't be alarmed; I plan on living for a long time yet. I just want to be ready when I pass and ensure that the people I care about have fewer logistical concerns during an incredibly stressful time.
>
> I care about you, and you matter to me. Let's talk about this soon — when works for you for a phone call?
>
> Be well.
>
> [Your name]

KEY FACTS ABOUT YOU

Full legal name: _____
Aliases or other names you go by: _____
Name you wish to be used in your obituary: _____

Gender: _____
Your pronouns: _____

Date of birth: _____
Birthplace: _____

Primary address: _____
_____

Additional address: _____
Relevant details about this address: _____
_____

Additional address: _____
Relevant details about this address: _____
_____

Current marital status: _____
Spouse or partner, if currently partnered: _____
Partner's email: _____
Partner's phone number: _____

Additional personal details: _____
_____
_____
_____
_____
_____
_____

KEY CONTACTS IN CASE OF EMERGENCY

If you were to pass suddenly, who would you **want** to know immediately, and who else **needs** to know immediately?

Closest Relatives

Name: _____
Relationship: _____
Contact Information: _____

Name: _____
Relationship: _____
Contact Information: _____

Name: _____
Relationship: _____
Contact Information: _____

Children/Dependents

Name: _____
Relationship: _____
Contact Information: _____
Who Should Care for them: _____
Location of Care Directives: _____

Name: _____
Relationship: _____
Contact Information: _____
Who Should Care for them: _____
Location of Care Directives: _____

Life Insurance

Company: _____
Account Number: _____
Contact Information: _____

Landlord/Morgage Lender

Name/Company: _____
Account Number: _____
Contact Information: _____

Employer

Name: _____
Address: _____
Supervisor or HR Liaison: _____
Contact Information: _____
Additional Professional & Employment Information: _____
_____

Doctor

Name: _____
Specialty/Practice: _____
Contact Information: _____
Additional Medical Information: _____
_____

Clergy or Counselor

Name: _____
Contact Information: _____

Attorney in Charge of Estate

Name: _____
Practice: _____
Contact Information: _____

Local Friends or Relations to Assist with Funeral Planning

Name: _____
Relationship: _____
Contact Information: _____

Name: _____
Relationship: _____
Contact Information: _____

Name: _____
Relationship: _____
Contact Information: _____

Notes about these individuals' connections to you, personalities, or communication styles that would impact how someone should communicate with them in a time of crisis: _____
_____
_____
_____
_____
_____
_____
_____
_____

FUNERAL INVITATION & NOTIFICATION LIST

Name: _____
Phone Number: _____
Email: _____
Address: _____
Connection to you: _____

Name: _____
Phone Number: _____
Email: _____
Address: _____
Connection to you: _____

Name: _____
Phone Number: _____
Email: _____
Address: _____
Connection to you: _____

Name: _____
Phone Number: _____
Email: _____
Address: _____
Connection to you: _____

Name: _____
Phone Number: _____
Email: _____
Address: _____
Connection to you: _____

Name: _____
Phone Number: _____
Email: _____
Address: _____
Connection to you: _____

Name: _____
Phone Number: _____
Email: _____
Address: _____
Connection to you: _____

Name: _____
Phone Number: _____
Email: _____
Address: _____
Connection to you: _____

Name: _____
Phone Number: _____
Email: _____
Address: _____
Connection to you: _____

Name: _____
Phone Number: _____
Email: _____
Address: _____
Connection to you: _____

Additional Information:
_____
_____

info@deathprojectmanager.com | deathprojectmanager.com

IMPORTANT DOCUMENTS:
SAVING YOUR LOVED ONES FROM LOGISTICAL HEADACHES

We recommend you start a **hard copy file of original documents** to accompany this Workbook. We suggest using a binder with multiple tabs or a box to contain more extensive paperwork.

Documents you should gather:

1. Will — executed by lawyer and signed by witness
    - If you do not have a will, consider who should be the executor of your estate and what you would like to happen to your:
        - Personal residence
        - Car
        - Household and personal effects
        - Personal papers and correspondence (will these go to a friend, relative, archive, or should they be disposed of?)
        - Cash
        - Children
    - Consider working with a financial advisor (refer to napfa.org as a resource) or an estate attorney (refer to nolo.com/lawyers/estate-planning) for complex estates.
    - If your assets are simple (no owned property, no major debts), consider using a will template for your state (refer to joincake.com/marketplace) and having it signed by two witnesses.
2. Letter of instruction[2]
3. Birth certificate
4. Social security card

---

[2] A "cheat sheet" of your estate with no legal authority, which serves as a clear explanation for your executor. Refer to investopedia.com/articles/retirement/08/letter-of-instruction.asp

5. Copy of driver's license or state ID
6. Passport
7. Life insurance information
8. Printouts of financial accounts, including retirement and/or pension information
9. Debtor information (debts you have incurred and/or debts others owe to you)
10. Health insurance or Medicare/Medicaid information
11. Any other insurance paperwork (home, car, personal property, etc.)
12. Medical directives[3], power of attorney paperwork, and living wills (refer to join-cake.com/advance-directives)
13. Lists of current medications and details of medical care (additional prescription information, names and contact information for your doctors and their specialties)
14. Marriage license
15. Divorce paperwork
16. Child adoption paperwork
17. Citizenship papers
18. Diplomas
19. Military records
20. Lease or mortgage paperwork
21. Deeds to properties you own
22. Location of burial plot if already purchased

---

[3] Advanced care directives articulate your desired medical care if you become unable to speak for yourself.

23. Bills related to property (utility account information, etc.)
24. Vehicle paperwork (title and insurance information)
25. Pet adoption and medical paperwork
26. Investment paperwork
27. Business ownership paperwork
28. Monthly donations to charitable organizations
29. Paperwork related to active volunteer and board service
30. Login information for digital assets (social media accounts, password managers)
31. Letters to loved ones

Notes
_____
_____
_____
_____
_____
_____
_____
_____
_____
_____
_____
_____
_____
_____
_____
_____
_____

Notes

TO DO LIST FOR LOVED ONES

In the immediate wake of your passing, there will be a lengthy list of tasks your loved ones will need to complete.

Please review and add items below, as relevant to you.

- ☐ Contact the Coroner's office to purchase at least 10 copies of the death certificate. The following action items often require a death certificate to complete, and the certificates are rarely returned after processing.
- ☐ Connect with a local funeral home about cremation, an institution for donation to science, or a designated funeral care provider.
- ☐ Set dates and times for the funeral, reception and visitation (if applicable). Contact those on the funeral invite list with a set of funeral expectations (e.g., colors to wear, songs to sing) and the nature of the service (e.g., a religious ceremony, nontraditional service).
    - Include a message instructing where to share condolences or, if applicable, where donations may be made in lieu of flowers.
        - Arrange for someone to remain at home for security during funeral services.
- ☐ Submit obituary to local newspapers.
- ☐ Connect with landlord about vacating the property and final rent payment.
- ☐ Contact an attorney for legal advice.
- ☐ Consult the will to set aside specific property for specific loved ones, as stipulated.
- ☐ Donate remaining clothes, art, etc. to a local charitable organization.
- ☐ Submit a change of address form to divert mail.
- ☐ Cancel bills (e.g., renter's or mortgage insurance, internet, utilities, cell provider).

info@deathprojectmanager.com | deathprojectmanager.com

- ☐ Determine if vehicle(s) should be sold or donated, or if ownership should be transferred.
- ☐ Cancel car insurance and AAA membership.
- ☐ Rehome pets.
- ☐ Close or transfer balances in financial accounts (e.g., bank accounts, credit cards, savings accounts, retirement accounts).
- ☐ Contact employer HR for information regarding insurance policies, and retirement accounts.
- ☐ Contact CPA, financial advisors, and business associates.
- ☐ If drawing social security, contact nearest Social Security office.
- ☐ Pay taxes.
- ☐ Send thank you notes and acknowledgements.

Other tasks relevant to you:

_____
_____
_____
_____
_____
_____
_____
_____
_____
_____
_____
_____
_____
_____
_____
_____

Notes

Notes

Notes

Notes

What would you like to practice more regularly as a result of completing this workbook? Schedule time on your calendar to do so for the next three months.

_____
_____
_____
_____
_____
_____
_____
_____
_____
_____
_____
_____
_____

Who would you like to be in contact with more regularly, or differently, as a result of completing this workbook? Schedule time to connect with them repeatedly for the next three months.

_____
_____
_____
_____
_____
_____
_____
_____
_____
_____
_____
_____

CLOSING REFLECTIONS

What have you gained from going through this process?

What challenges have you faced throughout this process?

Review your notes and goals from earlier in this workbook. How have things changed?

Review the preceding sections in this workbook. Make sure to add additional tasks and contacts that occur to you when reviewing these sections.

What are you proudest of, and why?

Do your loved ones know all of the above?

If you wrote your obituary today, what would it say?

What causes do you believe in?

What causes have you previously believed in, and why?

Do you plan to recognize any of these causes in your will or as a donation opportunity in lieu of flowers for your funeral?

What beliefs from childhood do you still hold, and why?

WHAT DO YOU WANT YOUR LEGACY TO BE?

How do you want to be remembered?
_____
_____
_____
_____
_____
_____
_____
_____

How do you think you will be remembered?
_____
_____
_____
_____
_____
_____
_____
_____

In what ways have you changed the most over time?
_____
_____
_____
_____
_____
_____
_____
_____

info@deathprojectmanager.com | deathprojectmanager.com

What do you believe in?
___

What is your motto? Or, what phrase do you say most often?
___

How would you like these memories and ideas expressed at your funeral?
___

What is the biggest challenge you have overcome?
_____
_____
_____
_____
_____
_____

What is your favorite memory?
_____
_____
_____
_____
_____
_____

Describe a time when you felt the most joy.
_____
_____
_____
_____
_____
_____

What is your most cherished possession, and why?
_____
_____
_____
_____
_____
_____

THE FUNERAL:
HELPING PEOPLE SAY GOODBYE TO YOU

WHO ARE YOU?

When you think of yourself, what are the top five descriptions that come to mind?

1. _____
2. _____
3. _____
4. _____
5. _____

When your closest loved ones think of you, what are the top five ways they would describe you?

1. _____
2. _____
3. _____
4. _____
5. _____

info@deathprojectmanager.com | deathprojectmanager.com

Advanced Care Directives

The National Hospice and Palliative Care Organization's Guide to States' Advance Care Directives (refer to nhpco.org/patients-and-caregivers/advanced-care-planning/advanced-directives/downloading-your-states-advanced-directive) is a helpful resource to read and complete with loved ones.

Please note that some variance exists among states' Advanced Care Directives. Some guides, such as 5 Wishes, have Advance Care Directive templates that are usable in 42 states and the District of Columbia (refer to fivewishes.org/docs/default-source/Samples/five-wishes-sample.pdf).

End of Life Care Options

To learn more about your options as you approach the end of your life, consult the National Institute on Aging's Guide to End of Life Care (refer to nia.nih.gov/health/providing-comfort-end-life).

Notes

_____
_____
_____
_____
_____
_____
_____
_____
_____
_____
_____
_____
_____

If you have a primary care doctor, do they know about these beliefs?

Have you completed Durable and Medical Power of Attorney paperwork?

Have you prepared a Living Will?

If you were to suffer a serious and permanent brain injury and become brain dead or comatose, do you have a threshold for how serious the effects would need to be before you would want to change your goals for care?

_____
_____
_____
_____
_____
_____
_____
_____
_____
_____
_____
_____
_____

What do you want your loved ones to know about your End of Life Care preferences?

_____
_____
_____
_____
_____
_____
_____
_____
_____
_____
_____
_____
_____

DECISIONS TO MAKE, DISCUSSIONS TO HAVE

Do you have any strongly held values or beliefs that would influence how medical decisions might be made at the end of your life, or in case you become unable to make decisions for yourself?

If you are incapacitated, who will make decisions on your behalf? Do they know this?

PETS

This is the last nice thing you get to do for your other loved ones. Include adoption and medical paperwork with hard copy documents.

Pet's Name: _____
Birth Year: _____
Medical Conditions: _____
Veterinarian Contact Info: _____
Care Instructions: _____
_____
_____

Pet's Name _____
Birth Year: _____
Medical Conditions: _____
Veterinarian Contact Info: _____
Care Instructions: _____
_____
_____

Pet's Name: _____
Birth Year: _____
Medical Conditions: _____
Veterinarian Contact Info: _____
Care Instructions: _____
_____
_____

Notes
_____
_____
_____

Login Information

Site: _____
Username: _____
Password: _____
Action to take: _____

Site: _____
Username: _____
Password: _____
Action to take: _____

Site: _____
Username: _____
Password: _____
Action to take: _____

Site: _____
Username: _____
Password: _____
Action to take: _____

Site: _____
Username: _____
Password: _____
Action to take: _____

Site: _____
Username: _____
Password: _____
Action to take: _____

How would you like your social media accounts managed after you pass?
_____
_____
_____
_____
_____
_____
_____
_____

What message would you like shared when you pass?
_____
_____
_____
_____
_____
_____
_____
_____
_____
_____
_____

Should any of these accounts post a copy of your obituary?
_____
_____
_____

Have you created a Facebook Memorial Page? (refer to facebook.com/help/1506822589577997)
_____
_____
_____

Should any of these accounts be closed in your passing?

Do you want any social media accounts kept open when you die?

If you choose to keep your digital accounts open after you pass, who will be responsible for maintaining them? Do they know your password(s), and have you designated them as a user that these accounts can transfer to?

SOCIAL MEDIA & DIGITAL ASSETS

What level of privacy — online and off — matters most to you?

_____
_____
_____
_____
_____
_____
_____
_____
_____
_____
_____

What digital accounts do you currently have? Think about social media as well as email, electronic payment accounts (including cryptocurrency), online photo albums, and online forums (such as Reddit).

_____
_____
_____
_____
_____
_____
_____
_____
_____
_____
_____
_____
_____
_____
_____

Notes

Catherine founded Death Project Manager to start conversations about mortality and help people get organized to face the inevitable. For more information, visit deathprojectmanager.com or follow @deathprojectmanager on Instagram.

Amy Burek is a printmaker and book artist who self-publishes her own work under the imprint Awkward Ladies Club. Her work can be found at awkwardladiesclub.com or on Instagram under the handle @awkwardladies.

Chute Studio is a collaborative Risograph studio created to expand publishing practices and print service offerings beyond individual press projects, Find out more at chutestudio.com. Follow @ohchute on Instagram for studio updates and new releases.